Seco
Lunatics

Hot Tips for Keeping your Second Born Child out of Prison
(and baby book)

Jimothy Williams

ISBN: 978-0-9905928-4-6

DEDICATION

To my second born, who taught me how to fight for my life.

ACKNOWLEDGMENTS

Thank you to my bed for being a comfortable place to rest after fighting for my life all day.

FIRSTBORNS VS. SECOND BORNS

Understanding the Differences

If you're reading this, you have at least two children, or you will soon.

A second born child is a child you either decided to have or nature decided to gift you after your first.

Firstborn Children

Chances are you have a firstborn who came out of the womb already potty trained, playing the violin, and spouting math facts. This child was so easy and good that you thought you were a fantastic parent (wrong).

Your firstborn's first words were to tell you the importance of saving for college.

They said, "I love and appreciate you, mommy and daddy' at three months of age and never had a tantrum in their life except for one time when they were sick.

Your firstborn does not gravitate toward trouble because negativity scares them. If you were to tell them to go to "timeout," they would have no idea what that is or how to get there because they've never been.

On the off chance that your firstborn does misbehave, a simple
raised eyebrow would send them into 40 days and 40 nights of deep lamentations.

Knowing that you are upset at them would ruin your firstborn's life. Yelling is unnecessary and would rip their soul in half.

At 6 pm on the dot, firstborns make themselves a balanced dinner, then draw a bath before ironing their pajamas and putting them on. They then brush their teeth twice, floss, read themselves a story and say goodnight to the family.

In their free time, firstborn children like to draw with colored pencils, laminate their awards, write letters to the elderly, and volunteer to bottle feed orphaned raccoons.

When they aren't playing, they usually are working a part-time job by age six to help the family make ends meet.

Firstborns are typically easy children. They are not like this because of who you are; they are like this because nature understands that to populate the earth, there needs to be a gateway child. This gateway child lulls their parents into a false sense of competence and tempts them to have more.

Parents think, "Wow this is so easy! What are those other parents talking about? We are better than them. We know things. We know discipline. Let's have another."

This is when your second born child will cannonball into your life.

SECOND BORN CHILDREN

Second-born children come out of the womb singing, "Last Resort" by Papa Roach. They had already been singing it in the womb and come out screaming the lyrics in your face while playing air guitar on their own placenta.

They are excited to be born and have people to wreck.

Your second born's first, second, and third words are either "no" or maniacal laughter. Before your second born knows what "no" means, they will say it because they like how it feels to say it.

"No" is who they are.

"No is who they want to be.

Sometimes your second born will say "No" when they actually mean "yes and punish you for not understanding.

By age two, the average second born is averaging 140 tantrums per half hour. This is a conservative estimate and depends on the amount of Pop Tarts in their system. The more Pop Tarts, the fewer tantrums.

Common reasons for second-born tantrums include:

- being asked to wear pants
- -being asked to wear a diaper
- -being asked to put on any clothes whatsoever

- eye contact
- being spoken to
- being breathed on
- being thought of
- being too close or too far from them

Second-borns gravitate toward chaos and drama because trouble is their lifeblood. They don't want peace; they want problems.

Second-borns do not hear things said in a regular tone of voice but yelling at them activates their fight or flight (mostly fight). Try grunting and pointing at things to keep them calm.

SAMPLE DAILY SCHEDULE

Second borns wake up angry and irritated that the sun rose without checking with them first.

If your second born wakes up in a good mood, it will cause them to hit the ground running with an energy level unseen in human beings but common in sheepdogs.

Second borns spend their days looking for adventure. If they cannot find it, they create it.

At 6 pm on the dot, second borns decide they don't like dinner whether or not they have seen it. Despite having voracious appetites and always being hungry, second borns do not enjoy mealtime because it involves sitting down.

After physically ripping up their dinner with their hands and eating maybe 6-7 bites, second borns will prowl the house looking for someone to fight with or scare.

By bedtime, your second born's face will be either streaked with tears or will be excited in a way that frightens you.

Second born children either do not sleep or sleep deeper than anyone else in the family. Anything in between is very rare and should be reported to science.

In their free time, second borns enjoy shredding paper, removing clothing items, hacking/destroying electronics, breaking toys, and emotionally exhausting their loved ones.

Second born children are not bad. They are simply built for wartime and not peace. Knowing and understanding how to keep your second born child safe and productive will be essential in your plan to keep them out of jail.

It can be done. Welcome to your journey.

ELISA, AGE 8

BY JOY, MOM

My first child, Kate, is so timid. She has a quiet stubbornness about her but would rarely put up a fight about anything. I vividly remember her first and only tantrum. It was at her third birthday party and the next day she came down with the flu.

The only time she acts out is when she's sick or something is very wrong. I thought it was because I read the book "Happiest Toddler on the Block" and fed her organic food.

Her sister Elisa was born when she was 3 1/2 after a very short labor. The first sound she made wasn't really a cry, it was more of an irritated sigh as if to say, "Was any of that even necessary?"

Since her birth, I have been annoying her every day of her life. Everything annoys her actually.

When she was two, I was convinced she might have a hearing problem because she was not responding to her name. Turns out, she was just ignoring me. I paid money to find that out.

Elisa has humbled me in many ways. I learned that I actually am a yeller! I had no idea. Elisa gives me many opportunities to practice patience and mindfulness every day.

Hot Tips for Keeping your Second born Child out of Prison

Tip #1 Know it's not your fault

Second borns were designed for war times. God knew there had to be different types of people for different situations in life.

Firstborns are meticulous people, maybe riddled with anxiety, maybe not, but we can agree that they are generally organized and enjoy sitting by the window with a cup of tea as early as 14 months old.

Second borns dream of being able to break a window and get away with it.

We can't all be accountants. We need soldiers who will run into a battle without thinking twice. These are second borns. If in the future your country finds itself in war, it will be the second borns grabbing the AK-47s and grenades.

Second borns are naturally fearless and crave a challenge. You may have noticed this by the reckless way they play in the jungle gym.

Personal safety is not on the radar of a second born at all. Not even a blip. Most of what they do is to maintain the adrenaline rush they were born with.

Your second born's nature may be problematic for you and your furniture.

No No Items For Your Home

1. Matches
2. Lighter fluid
3. Acetone
4. Permanent marker
5. Easily accessible scissors or clippers

Journal Prompt

Date:

What scares you most about your second born? Do you have homeowner's/renter's insurance?

Quiz

Second Born Facts

Age.................Date.................

My favorite movie is ______________________

My favorite television show is ______________________

My favorite drink ______________________

My favorite song is ______________________

My favorite book is ______________________

My favorite food is ______________________

Am I feeling positive? ______________________

My dream job is ______________________

Did I break anything today? ______________________

The most important thing to me is ______________________

HENRY, AGE 6

BY NICHOLAS, DAD

When Henry was born, our oldest was 18 months old. We were eager to have a second child because we'd had such an easy time with Henry's older brother Sam.

Henry was born with a smirk on his face and eyes I can only describe as crazy, but I chalked it up to his pupils adjusting to the light.

The look in his eyes never went away and is still there.

Henry wakes up every day and chooses violence, but to him, life is a fun game.

Last year, we went to Thanksgiving dinner at my employer's home. Sometime before the meal, Henry went into the kitchen and ate the stuffing out of the turkey. He also gnawed almost entirely through a turkey leg.

My wife caught him trying to hide the turkey leg in his pants. When she asked him why he'd done all of this he said, "I was hungry."

We said nothing, and everyone blamed the dog, but I believe they knew because Henry was so greasy he shone like a freshly waxed car. We have not been invited back since.

Tip #2 Try to see the positives.

Understand that your second born's nature can prove handy in cases where your timid firstborn may need to be defended.

If a child is bothering your firstborn at the park, it will be your second who will drop-kick the offending child into the next zip code before you can even cross the grass.

Second borns are also very observant and intuitive.

Firstborn children take whatever you say at face value. They are naturally trusting and respect authority.

Second borns know that everyone lies including their parents. If they catch you in one, they will immediately call you out and challenge your right to tell them anything again, ever.

With this commitment to the truth and justice, maybe your second born will be a judge or a public defender.

It's good to stay hopeful and positive about your second born's future. Pray over them every night.

Program your second born for success by saying things like, "If you believe it, you can achieve it."

Make sure your second born understands this phrase applies to things like wanting to be a teacher and not seeing if they can jump off the roof and live.

Journal Prompt

Date:

Name a death-defying feat your second born has attempted lately:

____

____

____

____

____

____

____

Tip #3 Do not let your second born catch you slipping.

Both firstborns and second borns are always watching, but second borns will use the intel they collect in subversive ways.

You may walk into the living room to see your second born eating a King Sized Snickers Bar and ask, "Where did you get that King Sized Snicker's Bar?"

Your second born will respond, "I saw you put them in the pantry behind the cans of peas, plus you said I could have a snack and you eat one alone in the pantry every day at 3:05 pm. I know because I can smell the chocolate on your breath."

In this response, your second born has challenged your status as alpha by 1) letting you know they found your stash, 2) letting you know they have found a loophole in the snacking policy, and 3) shaming you for your secret candy consumption.

Show no fear or shame, as this will strengthen your second born.

Journal Prompt

Date:

What is your second born's favorite non-lethal activity?

____

____

____

____

____

____

____

____

THIS OR THAT: SECOND BORN

Ask your second born to choose

Fire	Water
School	Park
Cereal	Candy
Milk	Juice
Running	Sitting
Pants	Naked
Yelling	Talking

Tip #4 Show no weakness, shock, or fear when your second born attempts to dominate you. The key is to outmaneuver them. This is chess, not checkers.

"Dear Jimothy,

My second born slapped me the other day, and I felt it in my soul. Am I still the parent?"

-Ben

Dear Ben,

The moment you got face checked by your second born, you were no longer the parent; you became the child. But as you recovered, you resumed your role as alpha. Learn to spot your second born's windup before they swing and duck or catch their hand mid-air. You gotta be quicker. We all learn with time.

Tip #5 Don't make them a middle child.

If for whatever reason you decided to have a third child, your second born is now a middle child which will intensify their propensity toward violence.

Much is said about the nature of middle children, but they are very simple to understand.

A middle child is a second born filled with an impossible amount of burning hot rage.

What was already an unstable situation, having a second born, has been exponentially destabilized by adding a baby.

The jealousy and anger your middle child has at being dethroned as the baby of the family cannot be understated.

Second-born children are very cute. They are exceptionally beautiful. Most agree this is because God is making up for how they act.

Between the attention a second born gets for their angelic looks and their otherworldly behavior, they are constantly in the spotlight.

Sharing the stage with a baby they view as inferior is unacceptable to your second born.

Your second born will do their best to let you know how you have deeply wronged them by bringing this child into the family.

HAS YOUR SECOND BORN...BINGO
Slapped you
Peed outside
Eaten grass
Eaten paper
Shoplifted
Said a swear
Stripped in a public place
Run into the traffic
Run away from school

Journal Prompt

Date:

How do you plan to explain to all future children that they work for your second born? Write a rough draft here.

____

____

____

____

____

____

____

____

Tip #6 Do not attempt to tell your second born that the new baby is "theirs" because, in their mind, property can be legally destroyed by the owner.

Second borns think in terms of dominance and food chains. To them, this new child has usurped their place in the family.

This could have been acceptable if this baby had won their position in a battle such as a knife fight or a wrestling match. But the fact that this new child has become the center of attention and affection due to being small and cute will cause your second born to increase in warfare against the family as a means of retaliation.

The second born to middle-child transition is one most people never fully recover from.

You may have a coworker who counts how many doughnuts each person in the office takes from the communal box to make sure it is "fair" or feels the need to say things like, "I dislike babies."

These are more than likely middle children.

After making a middle child out of your second born you may notice more conflict when asking them to complete tasks such as eating breakfast or not fighting their teacher.

Know that these things are difficult for your second born, who is full of tumultuous emotions.

Tip #7 Understand that any children born after the second born now work for the second born.

Second born children enjoy being in charge. They view any and all children born after them as their subordinates and interns.

Babies of the family do not usually have the initiative or motivation to behave as wildly as the middle child but will admire their commitment to chaos and fall in line.

Do not interfere with your middle child's role as director of the life of all younger siblings. It is the natural order of things and will give your second born a sense of purpose.

You may notice at times during regular play that it appears as if the siblings younger than your second born are hostages. They are. If you feel the need to intervene, do so in a way that does not usurp your second born's new authority.

The first, second, and third-born ecosystem is fragile and must be respected. As in any jungle, there is a hierarchy and a very complex set of unspoken rules.

Let them settle their own problems. If it becomes violent, wait a minute to see what happens but intervene if they pick up weapons.

Second
Born Snack
RECIPE
PREP TIME: 10 MINUTES
COOK TIME: 0 MINUTES
SERVINGS: 1
INGREDIENTS:
2 doughnuts (any variety)
1 large head of cotton candy
3 tbsp of sprinkles
1 cup of Cinnamon Toast Crunch cereal
14 lollipops
PROCEDURE:
1. Mix all of the ingredients until combined
2. Present to your second born on a platter
3. Send the child to grandma's house

Tip #8 The average second born has the energy level of a high-ranking navy seal. If these energy reserves aren't used by bedtime, they will be directed toward pets, drapes, other children, and your face.

<u>Fun Non-Violent Activities For Your Second born</u>

The key to an activity being fun for your second born is that it

2) requires a lot of physical energy.

2) feels life-threatening.

Both of these elements need to be combined for a second

born to have a good time and feel complete.

Here are a few activities I as an unlicensed second born professional recommend:

6. Play centers and amusement parks: These are expensive but can be used in a pinch to help a Saturday pass faster. Read the establishment's insurance policy to understand how they respond to property damage.

7. Home Obstacle course: move any breakable or sharp edges (end tables, televisions) to create a clear space. Arrange couch cushions and pillows in a basic training-style obstacle course that your second born can run through over and over again. Encourage them to beat their best time. Bonus points if you can install a rock climbing wall, swing, or rope dangling from the side of the house

8. Nature: Try to live near the woods and release your second born into them regularly. They will find things to do. Encourage them to leave all sticks by the front door. Check their pockets for spiders and sharp rocks.

9. Bath: Water tends to calm all children but especially second borns. Give them empty plastic containers, spoons, and any other toys. Supervise them closely, especially if they are with other children they view as weaker.

Tip #9 Second born children enjoy feeling like their souls could be snatched at any time. They live for danger and like it when activities threaten their safety. To them, this is fun.

SCRIBBLE PAGE

(At one point or another, your second born may feel aggressive toward this book for no reason at all and may want to ruin a page. Let them have this one.)

Tip #10 Arguing is like a verbal obstacle course for second borns. Set a five-minute time limit.

Whether they realize it or not, second borns argue for sport. It's how they become experts at such a young age.

When they are young, their arguments are nonsensical. As they grow older, they learn to weave through complex comparisons and anecdotes until they don't have the strength to go on.

Keep the arguments to a five-minute maximum and don't be afraid to say, "Because I pay the bills."

It's not a cop-out. It's for sanity's sake.

Also, never argue with a two-year-old. You've already lost.

Journal Prompt

Date:

What's the biggest mess your second born has ever made? Did you clean it up or just put a towel over it?

Tip #11 Know that your second born can regulate their temper. They choose not to with you because they trust you not to yeet them into the ocean. See it as a compliment.

You may have noticed that your second born has a short temper.

If your second born is in the toddler stages, this anger will express itself over anything from how the waffle is cut up to the color of the cup they are given.

Rather than say, "Mother, I do not appreciate being offered a green cup when yesterday, I fell in love with the pink cup," your second born might launch it across the room.

This may terrify you because you imagine your child to be the type of person who, in a fit of rage, drives a tractor into an office building or goes viral losing their mind in a restaurant because their mashed potatoes had a single lump.

Only people very close to them will ever see this side of them. The rest will think you are lying.

Tip #12 Reward your second born as they show self-control

Second borns do begin to control their turbulent emotions somewhat as they grow. Others find socially appropriate careers in which they can take it out on people.

I have not had time to conduct an official survey, but believe **85-99%** of hockey players are second born children. The same goes for boxers and mixed martial arts fighters.

Reinforce positive behavior in your second born by rewarding them when you see them, say, not drop-kick their sibling for eating the last granola bar.

Good rewards for second borns include electronic time, cash, shiny rocks, non-toxic washable paint, and NOT SCISSORS.

Don't you ever give them scissors.

ASK YOUR SECOND BORN TO CREATE AN IDEAL GROCERY LIST

DATE: ___________

Tip #13 Scientists are working feverishly to understand the root cause of the second born child's angst and believe much of it comes down to them not being the firstborn.

While your second born child does not want the responsibility of being a firstborn, they do desire the title.

Paired with the fact that they are constantly disappointed by the lack of dessert being offered in the home and letdown by the number of opportunities to jump from very high places, this creates a shaky emotional environment inside of your second born.

You need to know second born children do admire their firstborn siblings for their organizational skills, general caution, and mysterious ability to not always be in trouble.

They wonder what such a lifestyle must feel like.

But at the end of the day, they are born to be wild.

Journal Prompt

Date:

Is your firstborn afraid of your second born? List some evidence.

Tip #14 Always attend fancy functions with a spouse or helper. If/when your second born loses control, you will then be able to physically remove them from the situation while the other person grabs your belongings and/or other children.

Second borns can snap over anything.

"What if I am at a wedding, graduation, or church?"

Lightly threaten your second born ahead of time. Remind them of your expectations ("you will break nothing and no one").

They will remember none of this and respond to stimuli with their animal instinct.

No need to worry about your firstborn in this situation.

Firstborns are just as horrified as you are when your second born creates a scene and will follow you dutifully to the car as you remove your shoeless child from the venue.

Tip #15 Second born children are natural leaders who take a dictator approach to friendship.

Once second borns begin school, they will notice that some children have their own ideas about how games are played. This may lead them to spiral down into confusion, anger, and spitting.

Hopefully, you don't have a biter.

Explain to your second born that they are in not in charge of everyone. They will not understand you, but at least you said it.

Your second born's friends will either enable and cheer on their antics or take on a younger child's role and follow them into adventures.

If there are any big problems, the school will call you.

Journal Prompt

Date:

If your second born were to take over a small country, would they rule with violence or love? Provide evidence.

____

____

____

____

____

____

____

Tip #16 Second borns are blunt and very concerned with injustices. If they believe something is unfair, whether done by a friend or a 38-year-old third-grade teacher, the person is getting called out.

Hopefully, this is not your second born's teacher's first rodeo. If you do happen to be assigned to a first-year teacher, practice pretending to be surprised when they email you.

If you have a particularly spirited second born, their teacher will probably assign your child additional tasks in the classroom to keep him or her busy.

Many second borns adopt an alternate firstborn personality at school, which may shock you come parent-teacher night. Don't be resentful. They're leading a double life and showing self-control.

Tip #17 School can be hard for second borns. You're their personal assistant now.

In the 11-17 age range, your second born child will be facing a more stringent academic life and rich social life.

This is when it is critical to keep an eye on your second born as they tend to go to school mostly to have a good time.

Check their backpacks to make sure there are books in there and not stuffed animals, slime, or your entire pantry of snacks.

Try your best to know about upcoming projects so you are not going to a 24-hour drugstore for volcano model supplies at 9 pm the night before an assignment is due.

I am not saying second borns are irresponsible, they just like to party.

Journal Prompt

Date:

Have any of your second born's grandparents hinted that they view their grandchild's behavior as a form of Divine revenge? How did this make you feel?

Tip #18 Never compare your second born to your firstborn.

Dear Jimothy,

Should I compare my second born to my firstborn to help motivate him to be calmer and make it to school on time with both shoes on?

- Randall

Dear Randall,

When deeply offended, a second born will see it as their duty to teach you to never do something again. Nobody likes being compared. If you do this, your son may never wear shoes again simply out of spite.

Tip #19 Your second born may bully your firstborn. It's ok.

An unexpected benefit of having a bold-as-a-gangster second born is that he or she will help your anxiety cat of a firstborn learn to deal with life.

Firstborns tend to fear their own shadows, getting in trouble, loud voices, and anything else that threatens their constant hunt for safety.

It's no accident your firstborn was gifted with a sibling who would thrive in a tropical jungle setting.

Your second born will see the weakness in their older sibling and may bully them just a little bit. Having to fight back against the harassment of their younger sibling will help your firstborn develop a voice, fighting skills, and a strong backbone.

They'll need this for the real world. Let them duke it out but be clear you won't be visiting the emergency room after 2 pm.

SECOND BORN MEAL PLANNER

MONDAY

Chicken nuggets with a side of chicken nuggets.
Apple slices (for decoration)

TUESDAY

Chicken tenders with a side of chicken nuggets.
Cucumber slices (for decoration)

WEDNESDAY

Chicken tenders with a side of dry cereal in a bag.
The scent of one orange.
Unexplained chocolate.

THURSDAY

Cereal with milk.
Eight slices of pizza.
A fruit.

FRIDAY

Air

Journal Prompt

Date:

How does our second born indicate he or she is hungry? (Growling, scratching, crying, searing rage, etc.) List their favorite foods.

Tip #20 Keep your second born well fed.

99.98% of the second born violence that occurs in your home is because the child is hungry.

Get ahead of your second born child's outbursts by keeping them topped off with fruit, carbs, and protein. Second borns sometimes pretend to be picky, but the truth is that most of them would eat plastic for the experience.

Second borns have voracious appetites and eat 3X as much as their other siblings by 2 months of age. Keep the pantry stocked and meals coming.

Half of the time, when they are angry or sad, they're hungry.

Second borns often don't know they are hungry. Leave a quesadilla and carrot sticks in their vicinity and observe what happens from a safe distance.

To get them to try new vegetables, tell them it's dangerous and you'd rather they didn't.

Watch them around sugar because they have no internal regulation system telling them their bodies would be in danger if they ate 15 doughnuts in 25 seconds.

Watch them.

Tip #21 Buy them craft supplies.

Second borns love to make a mess. They live for it.

You can either let them destroy $200 of makeup from Sephora and your entire house or give them a specialized set of craft supplies they can do whatever they like with.

A craft kit for a second born should contain: three different kinds of tape, at least four containers of glue (different colors), a set of markers, a set of crayons, child-proof scissors (two pairs), a carton of baking soda, a small jar of vinegar, buttons, paper, a full set of washable finger paints, a set of paint brushes, a tube of toothpaste, six toothbrushes, ten empty Tic Tac containers, a measuring tape, four empty cardboard boxes of various sizes, tin foil, a box of popsicle sticks, a glue gun (if age appropriate), 12 rocks, 8 pinecones, birdseed, a roll of heavy-duty string, a pencil, and a notepad.

When your second born desires to "craft" set them up outside on the grass or at the kitchen table in their underwear. Resist the urge to comment.

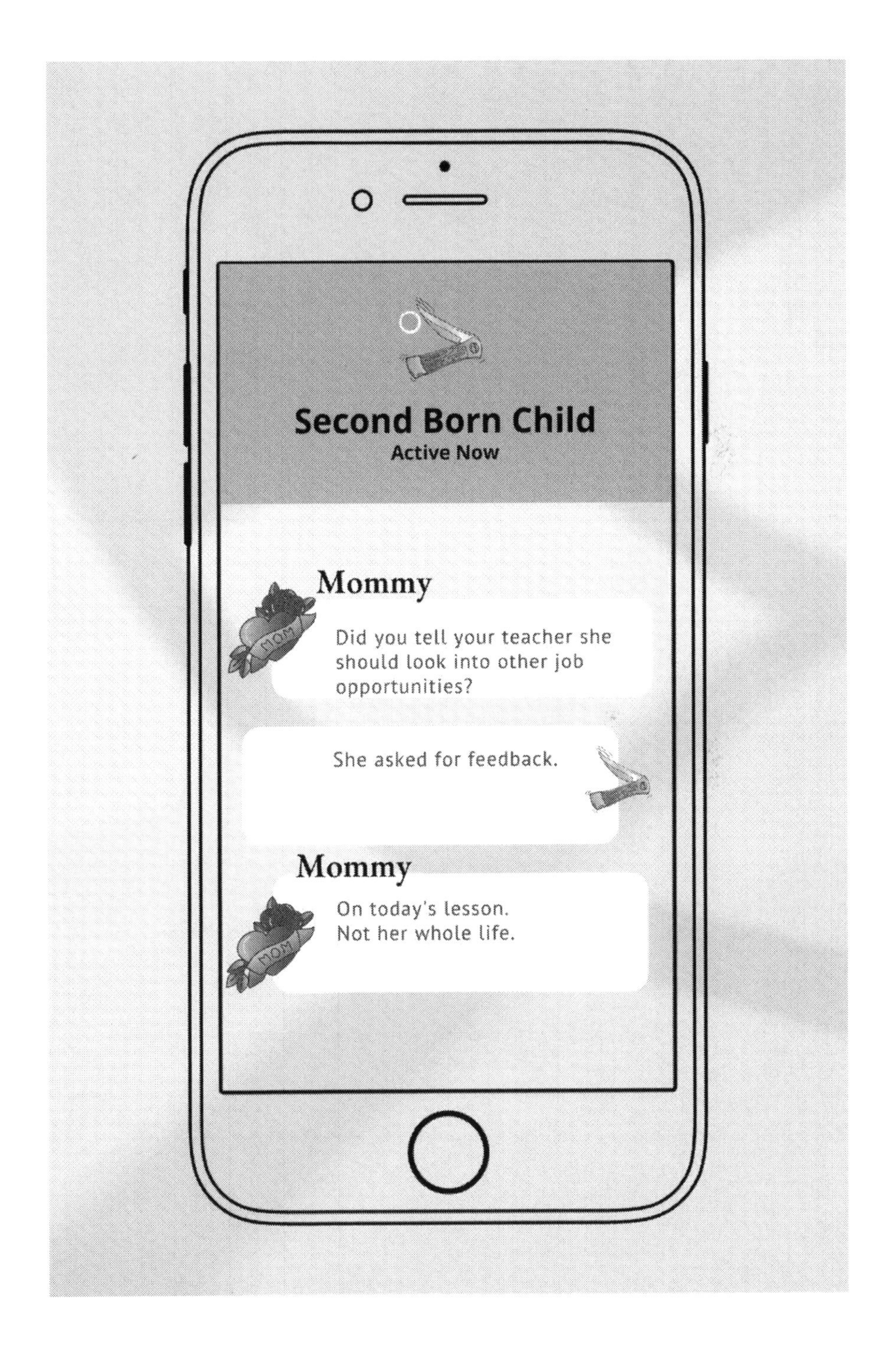
Second Born Child
Active Now
Mommy
MOM
Did you tell your teacher she should look into other job opportunities?
She asked for feedback.
Mommy
MOM
On today's lesson.
Not her whole life.

Journal Prompt

Date:

Second borns are blunt. What's the hardest truth yours has ever slapped you or someone else with?

Tip #22 Don't buy them expensive clothes.

Unless you like burning money, keep your second born's clothes cheap.

If your second born is running around in $30 polo shirts, you're going to run yourself ragged trying to keep them clean and out of trees.

Second borns need danger and messes to live. Thwarting their natural desire to come home from second grade looking like they've returned from war is only going to cause their chaos to come out in other ways.

Let your second born experience and release their monkey energy the way they were meant to.

If you can, give them the clothes their older sibling can't fit into anymore. If that's not possible, buy them $4 shirts and $6 pants from the cheapest store in your city.

Before you buy an item of clothing for our second born, ask yourself: "If this came home ripped down the back, smelling like an outhouse, and covered in Sharpie, would I be very upset?"

If yes, put it back.

Journal Prompt

Date:

Name one way your second born has made you a better person.

____

____

____

____

____

____

____

Second born Activity

Name: **Date:**

Ask your second born to draw a picture of themselves. If they're too young, trace their hand (this is their baby book after all).

Tip #23 Give them undivided attention.

I know you're busy. And exhausted. We all are. But even ten minutes can change a lot.

Second borns have both an inferiority and superiority complex. They live in a constant shadow of the perfect firstborn. And let's face it, they're almost always in trouble.

A lot of the attention they get is for doing the wrong thing. Ten minutes of asking your second born what they're making, doing, or thinking will light up their lives like you wouldn't believe.

Mix things up and show them how good positive attention can feel. Take them on a solo walk. Chat with them before bed. Let them help you in the kitchen alone.

It can be hard to do this when you've got other kids in the house, but carving out space where your second born doesn't have to shout to be heard will be a gift to them that doesn't cost a thing.

Tip #24 Don't take their insults personally.

Look. Some truly wild things will come out of your second born's mouth. Don't dwell on it.

Yes, you've got to let your second born know certain language won't fly. Consequences you follow through on are important unless you want to be picking them up from a Scared Straight day at the jail by age 11.

But know your second born's mouth works faster than their brain. Did they call you a "fat lard monster" or say "I wish you weren't my mommy?"

Second borns are actually super sensitive people and knowing you are hurt by what they said will impact them more than knowing you're angry.

Tell them they hurt your feelings. Make a consequence. Go in a corner and cry for a few minutes. Then get on with your life.

If you truly feel like you can't move on from what was said, you can always deduct an appropriate amount from their inheritance one day.

Tip #25 Laugh.

You don't need cable or to visit the comedy club: you have a second born child.

Second born children are undeniably hilarious. They are that friend from college whose antics you couldn't believe they got away with.

They're the class clown.

They're the wild card.

They are the life of the party.

Yes, they're a handful, and every day is like waking up to a surprise bag, but one day they will move out, so try to laugh.

Once they're asleep, think of the funniest thing they did that day or week. Tell your friends. Tell their grandparents.

And then go to bed. You'll need your energy for tomorrow.

Good luck.

ABOUT THE AUTHOR

Jimothy Williams is a father of 3+ kids. He enjoys the garage and his family, but not in that order.

Published by Hoodie and Latte Books

Read more at www.HoodieAndLatte.com